Unspoken Feelings Of A Firefly

jovan alitagtag

BookLeaf Publishing

India | USA | UK

Made with ❤ on the BookLeaf Publishing Platform
www.bookleafpub.in
www.bookleafpub.com

Dedication

For my wife,
my family, and
those who believe in me

Preface

This collection is not loud.
It does not boast or burn.
It glows—softly, steadily—
like faith in a storm,
like a question that waits years for an answer,
like a firefly in an open field
choosing to shine anyway.
These are poems born
from ambition and ache,
from names misheard and dreams misread,
from silence stretched thin over prayer.
A man still learning
that healing is a kind of light too,
and that some stories are written
not to impress,
but to remind us we're not alone
in the becoming.
If you find even one small light here—
hold it.
Let it walk with you a while.
—*Jovan B. Alitagtag, PhD*

Acknowledgements

To my wife—
thank you for seeing the poet in me before I ever did.
Your love, faith, and gentle push gave these poems their
first breath.

244

Is this real?
Still can't believe that I've got the deal.
I've got the deal and it was sealed
leaving my father, my pain I concealed.
I hugged him tight and never looked back
for I know the longing will attack.

Wait—can this be true?
Now, I do not know if I am sure.
It was a dream to go beyond horizon
but never thought it was a tough decision.
Thinking about the goal,
let's go from pole to pole!

On this journey, I will never stand alone,
as I face the greatest unknown.

Flight of Faith

To fly or not to fly, that is the question.

I was born a fighter,
never to surrender.
I grew up with nothing,
believing I could be something.
This is what I told to myself
when I see nothing on the shelf.
I live without silver spoon
a challenge I called a boon, not a wound.
It shaped me in to someone tough,
prepared me to face a world so rough.
"I can make it"—my heart would cry,
for I never believed in a fairy tale lie.
I was an outstanding teacher for years
yet now, no student is near to cheer
I left my courage, my dreams in sight,
never knowing I'd cry at night.
I was distant from the teacher I'd been,
yet I thank God—this is where I begin.

Returning to the question, my reply—
Yes, I flew, and now I soar high.

A Bridge of Dreams

Pursuing dreams across the sea,
A leap of faith was asked of me.
God heard my heart, He made a way,
Through I-Bridge, I found my stay.
Their hands reached out, so firm, so kind,
With every step, they walked behind.
From hopes once whispered in a prayer,
They built a path, they brought me there.

A brand-new world, a foreign shore,
New faces, cultures, dreams, and more.
Though challenges and doubts appeared,
I-Bridge stood strong, they calmed my fear.
Through homesick nights and changing skies,
Their constant care became my guide.
Their service wrapped in earnest grace,
Made every new step feel like place.

I always stand with thanks to give,
A stronger heart, a life to live.
I hold this journey in my hand,
A testament to where dreams stand.
Forever grateful, this is true—
God's faithful hand, and I-Bridge too.

When I Couldn't Forgive

I chased a dream with fire in my chest,
Believing I was chosen, guided, and blessed.
I thought that I found people I could trust—
But behind my back, they scattered dust.

Their words were poison, hidden in a smile,
Yet I stayed silent, walked that mile.
Months went by, I held my tongue,
Thinking silence meant I'd won.

I told myself I'd let it go,
That time had softened every blow.
But every time their name arose,
A hidden thorn beneath me froze.
I whispered prayers, I asked the Lord,
"Take this weight I can't afford."
I cried, "I've tried, I really did,"
But bitterness stayed where it hid.

And then one night, when I could barely pray,
The truth I'd buried came my way:
I hadn't truly let it go—
I just buried it beneath the show.

Not for their sake, but for my soul,
Forgiveness had to be the goal.
Not to excuse or make things right,
But to free my heart from endless night.
I saw myself through heaven's eyes,
Not as the victim, but unwise.
I hadn't walked the words I knew,
Hadn't shown what grace could do.
So, I stood not as the wronged, but flawed,
Asking mercy from my Lord.

Not for the anger I held too long—
But for failing to live as love made strong.
To love like Christ, to turn the cheek,
To kneel in strength when I felt weak.
I learned that healing starts inside,
Not with justice, but with pride set aside.
So here I am, with hands held high,
Not asking why—but asking try.

Try again to bless the pain,
To let compassion fall like rain.
And if forgiveness takes a while,
I'll walk each step with mercy's smile.

For though I stumbled, missed the mark—
God lit a lamp in the place so dark.

Thursday Night for His Life

Each Thursday night, our hearts ignite,
We gather close, in faithful light.
Far from the home we used to know,
God gave a place for us to grow.
With open arms we lift our songs,
We find the place where we belong.
In every laugh, in every tear,
His love is present, always near.
No ocean vast, no mountain high,
Can dim the praises that we cry.
Our bond was forged not by our hand,
But by the Lord's own perfect plan.
> Each week we rise with hearts set free—
> Thank You, Lord, for having this family.

I Live by the Skin of My Teeth

I was longing just to feel alive,
To ask what more awaits my tribe.
So I left behind familiar skies,
Chasing dreams with teary eyes.
Here I stand, across the sea,
A teacher in a land unknown to me.
I know my craft, I hold my ground—
Yet silence echoes louder than sound.
The classroom hums with restless air,
But in their eyes, I'm barely there.
I teach, I plan, I strive, I speak,
Still, it's myself I barely meet.

I am hurt.
I am wounded.
But it's not something I wish to flee—
It's something I carry carefully,
Proof that I am still becoming me.
Homesick days, where is my past?
The self I knew—did she not last?
I miss the language, laughter, light,
Where culture wrapped me warm and tight.

Here, I unlearn just to survive.
But in the ache, I feel alive.
It stings—it sings—this tangled grace,
To lose, to stretch, to find my place.
It's not defeat—it's something bright,
A fire born from inner fight.
I do not break; I bend, I grow—
With every no, a deeper "know."

I live by the skin of my teeth each day,
But I live—and that's enough to say.
Through loss, through longing, through quiet cries,
I rise again—with open eyes.

Becoming...SEVEN

They say when you reach year seven, something might break—
a heart, a rhythm, a vow you thought you'd never fake.
They whisper, "It gets rocky, you'll lose what you adore,"
but some hold on, and somehow, love becomes more.

This is my seventh, and I feel the same fear—
what if I've peaked? What if no one wants to hear?
The words stall now—once fluid, now unsure—
and I wonder—am I still me if I don't create like before?

But maybe the seventh is not an end—
maybe it's where real beginnings start to bend.
Not every flame is meant to blaze—
some quietly burn through their softest phase.
So here I write, unsure if I should stay—
but still, I write—becoming, anyway.

Someday, One Day

I still remember those younger days—
We'd scroll and dream in quiet ways.
Sharing posts on Tumblr threads,
Facebook hopes our hearts had said.

Photos of dates we longed to try—
Theme Park rides and Frappes high,
Couple shoes and movie nights,
Long car drives under city lights.

We called them dreams—someday, one day,
Whispers soft in a hopeful way.
You were my wish, my silent prayer,
To build a life with love to spare.

Now look at us—two years as one,
The dreaming done, yet just begun.
Little by little, truth takes form,
The simple things that keep love warm.

Still, I strive for what's ahead,
To live the vows, we softly said.
A better man, a husband, a heart that tries—
To give you love that never dies.

So here we are, hands intertwined,
With more to dream, more peace to find.
And though you've always deserved the best,
I pray I am your answered quest.

Just like *Bawat Daan* by Ebe,
And *Araw-Araw* by Ben&Ben,
No matter what we face or fear,
Through every step, I'll still be nearby.

My love will always choose to stay,
To guard our joy along the way,
And brave the storms that life may send—
With you, my love, my truest friend.

For you are my *Tadhana*, my guiding light,
In this *Once in A Lifetime* that feels so right.

Where You've Always Been

In the living room where we sat and shared our laughter
—that's my favorite place.
Because there, I know I'll always have a space.
You love me still, no matter the case.
And maybe I took it for granted,
believing you would always stay.

When I'm sad, you show up—quiet, but near.
When I'm frustrated, you listen to every nonsense fear.
When I'm mad, you don't turn away—
instead, you make me feel special in your own gentle
way.

As we continue this journey, I've come to realize:
I became so familiar, so comfortable with you,
that I took you for granted—
not knowing that those who love us the most
deserve the very best of us.

Grateful you stayed through all my seasons,
without judgment, and held me without needing reasons.
Your love was the light I couldn't see—
but now it shines clearly inside of me.

A Boy Who Cried, Now Praises God

Inside of me, a boy still hides,
With tears I never quite could dry.
I learned too young what sorrow means—
A silent scream, a heart that dreams.
I wore a smile to mask the pain,
The cheers would fade, replaced by rain.
My world went dim when light was gone—
The "home" I knew, forever drawn.

I blamed the Lord when all seemed lost,
Let go of faith, no matter the cost.
The weight I bore was far too wide,
No answers came, though questions cried.

Inside, a voice begins to rise,
Her words still echo, calm and wise:
"Have faith, my child, through rain or sun—
Trust in the Lord until you're done."

It's in my heart—my mother's grace,
And through her words, I found my place.
For through it all, He never strayed,
In silent love, He always stayed.

The boy who wept is now a man,
I lift my hands, as God once planned.
I walked back to the church she knew—
Not the same seat, but a heart made new.
And in that place her prayers remain—
A legacy born out of pain.

A Lighthouse

When darkness came, and shadows clouded my way,
You stood as light, a beacon through my night.
In grief's cold grip, you chased my fears away,
A lighthouse shining steady, pure, and bright.
Through sacrifice, you gave without a plea,
Ensuring we had all that we could need.
You taught me love, and how to truly see
The strength in kindness, planting hope as seed.
Your gentle hands have held my heart so dear,
Through every storm, you've never turned away.
Your steadfast love, a warmth that I hold nearby,
A flame that guides me through dismay.
    In life's vast sea, if I must choose one light,
    I'd choose you, my sister, my heart's true sight.

The Strength Beneath

The gap between us like a mountain high,
Yet I've learned from you, through every climb.
Not always perfect, but you are never shy,
Steady through struggles, no matter the time.
You are a mountain, with strength untold,
With peaks and valleys, both fierce and grand.
I've watched you rise, with courage bold,
Through every storm that you've had to withstand.
Impulsive, yes, your path's a winding trail,
Yet with each step, I've seen your truth unfold.
In your failures and triumphs, you prevail,
A force of nature, both gentle and bold.
    If I must choose again, through life's vast span,
    I'd still pick you, my brother, my mountain man.

Through the Cosmos, We Thrive

We were wanderers in a distant sky,
    Strangers adrift, stars passing by.
In the orbit of work, our paths aligned,
    Three rogue comets, one perfect design.
Nights were meteors, blazing and bright,
    Drinking through galaxies, chasing the night.
We laughed in the black of endless space,
    Spinning through dreams at a reckless pace.
But gravity pulled with a wiser hand,
    A whisper to anchor, a call to land.
We traded the stars for steady flight,
    From beers to books, from dusk to light.
Planets we built from sweat and dreams,
    Mapping new worlds with daring schemes.
You pushed, I soared, we pulled each other,
    Like moons in dance around one another.

Team Mercury — fast, fierce, and free,
Riding the edge of destiny.
Not just travelers of fleeting skies,
But constellation time can't be denied.
Companions in cosmos, lighting the way,
Team Mercury — forever we stay.

Tired of Becoming

I was taught that I have to be better than my yesterday—
compete with who I was, not anybody else.
But how can I, if my yesterday broke me...
not just once, not twice,
but so many times?

Every time I wake up,
I feel like there's a scoreboard on my face—
and it always shows zero points.
I feel like I'm in a game
I never chose to play.

Climb higher. Push harder. Smile wider.
That's what I've got to do.
And I realized—
no one asks if I'm tired.
No one asks if I'm getting any wiser.
They just say, "Hey, you're getting older!"

They cheer and clap when I win,
but why are they all silent when I bleed?

When I look in the mirror—
why doesn't it smile back?

Why does it feel like it measures... it mocks?
My reflection is fleeting.
I'm losing my face.
I can't...breathe.

How can you breathe
when your worth is measured
by how much more you can become?

Oh, shocks—
why does yesterday's triumph feel like a fading shadow?
And today? Today demands more.

Wait—who set this fire?
What is the cause?
Why is enough never enough?

When will I stop?
Can I rest?
Wait... is it rebellion to rest?
Why does stillness feel like shame?

To be honest—
I'm tired of fighting who I was
just to impress who I might be.

Cost of Craving

He chased the horizon,
    forever stretching,
    an endless pursuit
    to be more,
    to have more,
    to give more.

Each step was a promise—
to build, to grow, to rise—
but the roots beneath him weakened,
unseen in the rush.

He forgot the quiet whispers of his own soul,
drowned in the noise of striving.

In the mirror, a reflection changed—
hair thinned, skin worn,
a body bearing the toll of neglect.

Ambition had demanded it,
had taken and taken,
until all that was left was the echo of his own name.

And yet, he still ran...

Still reaching,
still grasping,
still forgetting the cost—
the man he had been,
the man he was losing.

Hope in the Waiting

Longing to touch the fruit of love
unceasing prayer is what's been done
nurturing the heart that's on the run
asking God when to see the dove
morning and night waiting...for the signs
yearning to see the sacred two lines
preparing for what is yet to come
uplifting the spirits is what can only be done
remembering His words brings calm
planting the seed...hoping to reap, even one
offering my all, still longing for a chance
strengthening the faith to have a stance
enduring uncertainty till it happen.

The Unfinished Portrait

I've captured moments, degrees in hand,
A bachelor's, master's, doctorate complete,
Each frame a triumph, every step so sweet,
Yet one dream waits—too far for me to land.
A family portrait, all together, stand—
A vision still unseen, a hope unclear.
In every frame, a gap I cannot fear,
A photo incomplete, not yet so grand.
Though joy fills my heart with all I've done,
A simple wish persists, and pulls me through—
To see us whole, beneath the setting sun,
A single shot where all my dreams come true.
    Until that moment, I'll continue true,
    Chasing that picture of a love that's new.

For the boy they once called "alitaptap"

They used to call him *alitaptap*,
a name made in jest,
but how could they know
he'd grow into the glow?

Why must I shine in darkness?
he once asked,
feeling the weight of quiet nights,
the ache of being unseen.
But the firefly answered:
Some lights are made for shadows,
not stages.

Why do I flicker—strong, then faint?
Because the firefly knows
even a pulse of light
can guide the lost.

Why do I feel so small
in a world so wide?
But the firefly flies anyway,
never needing to be big
to be bright.

Why do I carry so much
and still try to give?
The firefly glows
not for praise,
but because that's what it was born to do.

So, he walks on,
     not mocking the name
     but honoring it.
     For he is ALITAGTAG—
     flicker-born, faith-lit,
     a man who learned
     that even the softest light
     can answer the darkest questions.

Victor, Creature, Hamlet, & Me

I am Victor—
not the man who defied the heavens
with trembling hands and fevered pride,
but the son of a quiet lineage,
who gathers the broken tools of his fathers
and dares to build something better.
I do not chase lightning—
I chase peace,
the kind that was never passed down,
the kind I must forge with blistered palms
and a prayer beneath my breath.

I am also the Creature,
not made of bone and bolt,
but of late-night weeping and Sunday kindness,
stitched together by the gentle hands of a sister
who gave what little she had
to keep me from the cold.
I walk through crowds,
a believer still—
that we are born open-hearted,
that bitterness is a coat we learn to wear
when the world turns away.

But I am Hamlet, too.
At times I stand still,
surrounded by decisions
that tighten like thorns around my ribs.
I hear the whispers—
not of kings, but of ghosts
whose faces bear my name:
"Don't fail like I did."
"Stay small—stay safe."
"Why dream so big?"
Their grief clings to my spine
and makes my courage tremble.

So I move,
not as swiftly as fire,
not as boldly as prophets,
but I move.
I am the vessel, the shaped, the still-becoming—
ambitious, tender, torn.
And in this storm of silence and legacy,
a flame is kindled—not by me,
but by the One who sees beyond the dark.
I walk forward, not to escape my past,
but to heal it, step by step,
on the path God lays before me—not in haste,
but in trust.

to the kid i was once

to the kid i once was, full of wonder and fear,
i see you now through time so clear.
you held in tears and hid your cries,
but still you dreamed beneath those skies.

you stumbled forward, bruised but brave,
each scar you earned, a path you paved.
you didn't know how far you'd go,
but even then, your heart would glow.

i hope when we meet, eye to eye,
there's no regret, no need to lie.
just pride for all that we've been through,
a whispered, "look—we made it through."

no ifs, no buts, no shame to face,
just love, and peace, and full embrace.
a hug so tight, we both forgive—
and thank the boy who learned to live.

Becoming Again

I was aiming so high, but it left me with a sigh.
I kept dreaming at night, beneath a starry sky.
I was pleading with the Most High, asking why—
while quietly contemplating the meaning of this life.

As I look in the mirror, I see something's missing—
reflecting on where I've been, the person I had been—
questioning if I should push through, claiming I can
make it through,
hoping that one day, I'll see the person I wish I could be.

Maybe it reminds me—not everything is meant to stay.
I lost some parts of me along the way,
or left behind what I no longer need from yesterday—
to light the path, I was always meant to take.